BOOK 1

Toccatas

6 Impressive Solos for Piano

DENNIS ALEXANDER

The word toccata comes from the Italian word *toccare* (to touch). Such virtuosic pieces for the keyboard typically display the performer's technique. In my own teaching, I have discovered that piano students enjoy flashy, exciting toccatas that let them truly shine in recitals, competitions, and festivals.

In writing the toccatas for this collection, my goal was to motivate students to build speed and agility over a wide range of the keyboard. Each piece provides an opportunity to demonstrate such dexterity combined with musicality, characterization, and a genuine command of the instrument. In choosing titles for the toccatas, I decided to combine the word toccata with another musical term to help increase the musical vocabulary of students.

I hope that both students and teachers have fun with these pieces. Likewise, I would like to see audiences respond with enthusiastic applause coupled with shouts of "Bravo!"

Dennis Alexander

CONTENTS

Toccata alla breve	14
Toccata capriccio	2
Toccata concitato	20
Toccata fuoco	17
Toccata marcato	6
Toccata strepitoso	10

Dedicated to my friend and musical colleague Dr. Martha Baker-Jordan

Alfred Music
P.O. Box 10003
Van Nuys, CA 91410-0003
alfred.com

Copyright © 2020 Alfred Music
All rights reserved. Printed in USA.

No part of this book shall be reproduced, arranged, adapted, recorded, publicly performed, stored in a retrieval system, or transmitted by any means without written permission from the publisher. In order to comply with copyright laws, please apply for such written permission and/or license by contacting the publisher at alfred.com/permissions.

ISBN-10: 1-4706-4174-7
ISBN-13: 978-1-4706-4174-0

Cover art: Art resources courtesy of Getty Images

Toccata capriccio*

Dennis Alexander

*Capriccio = a piece in free form

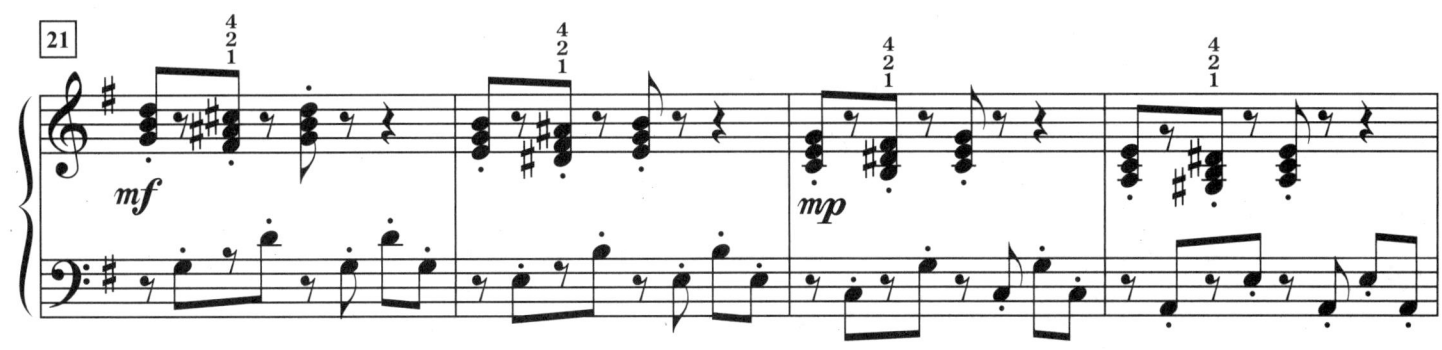
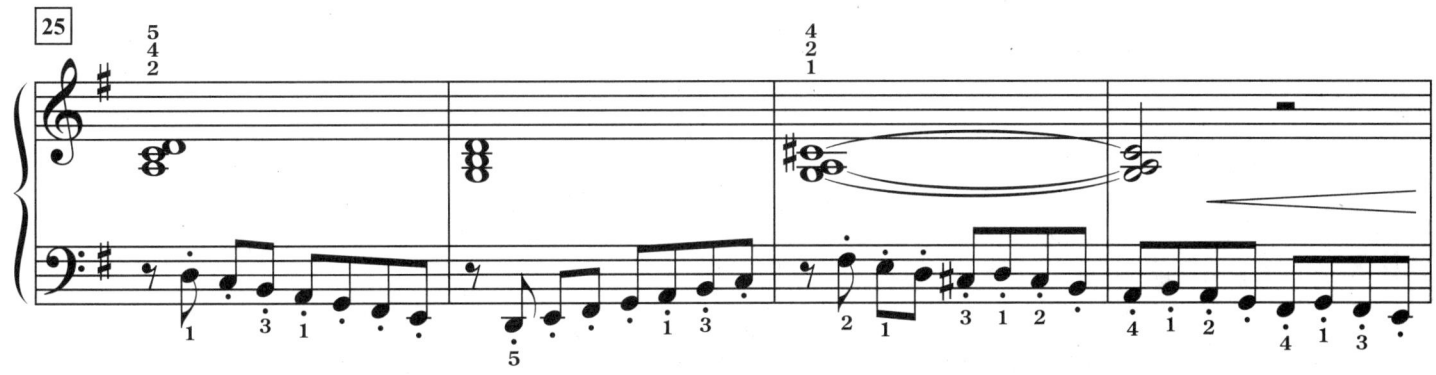
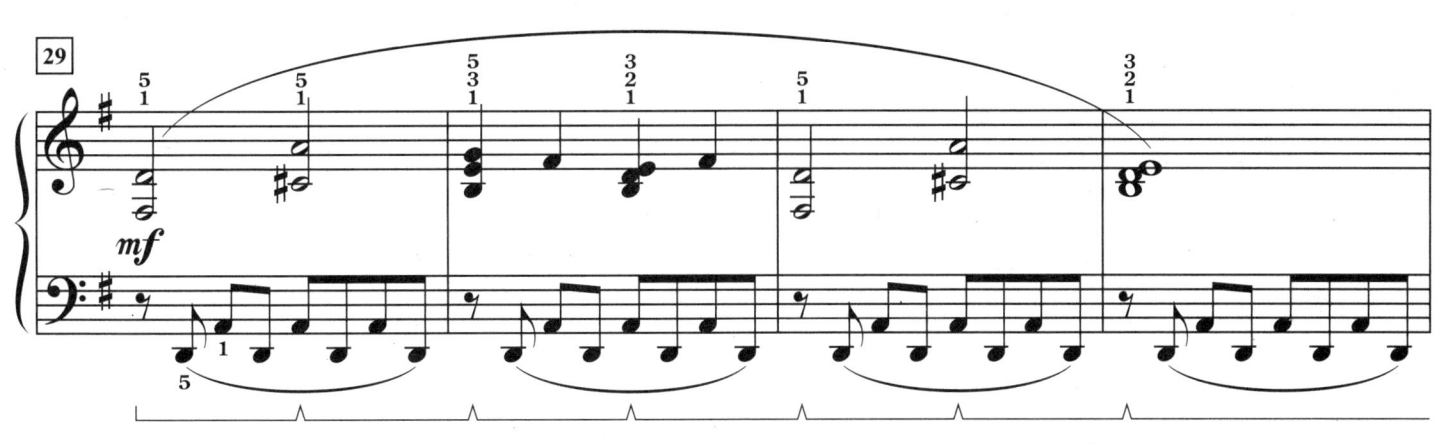

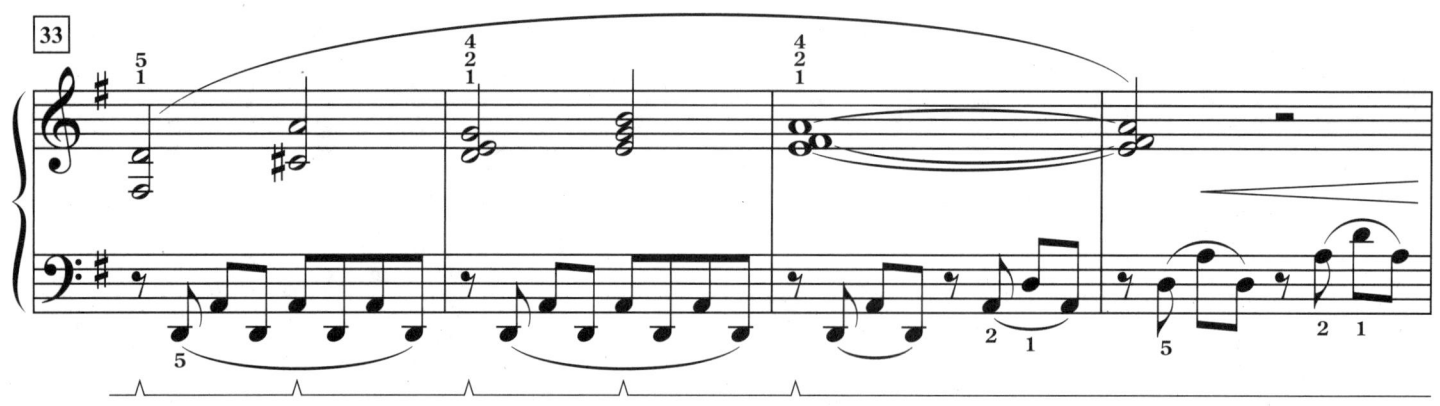
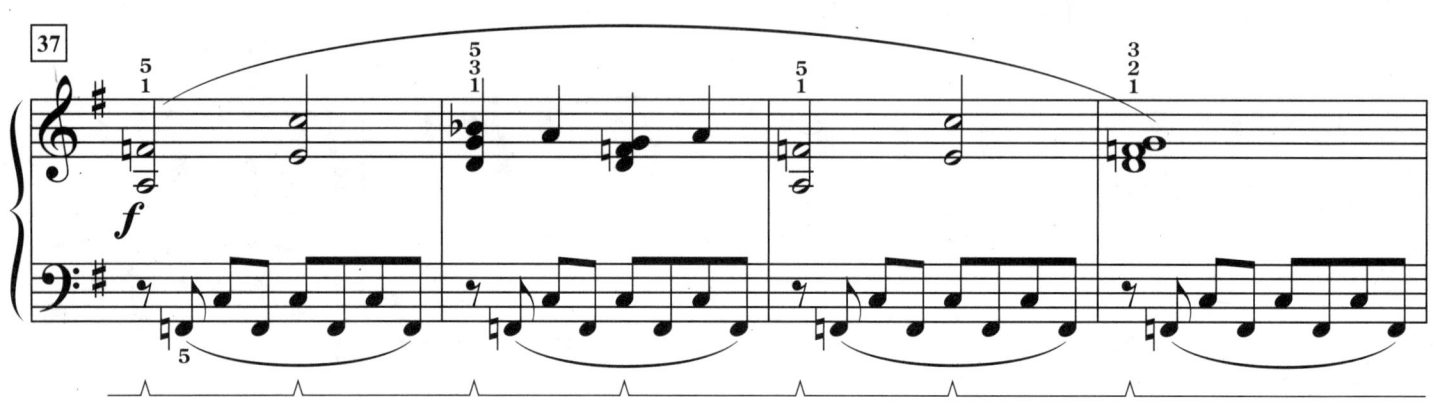
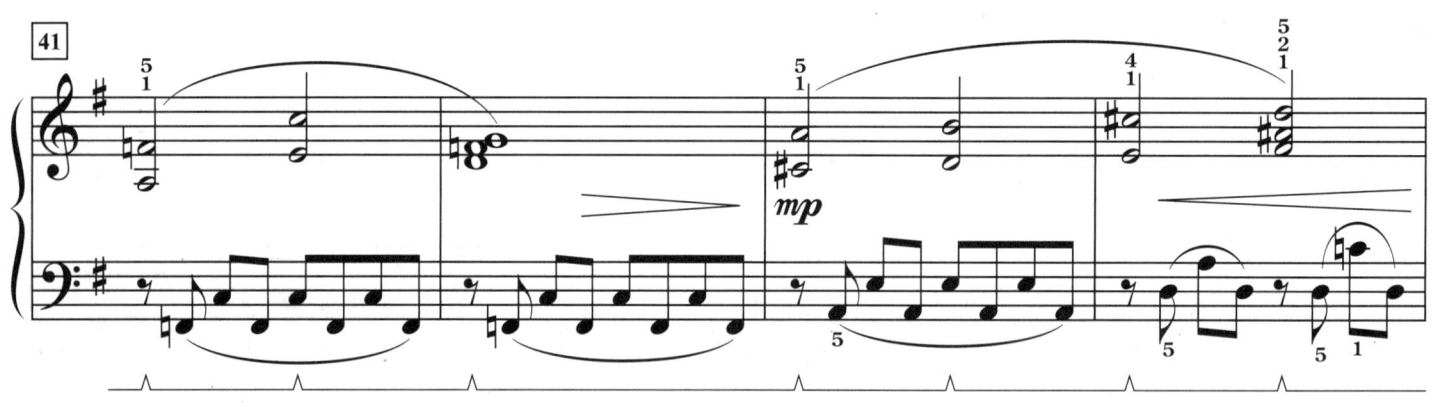

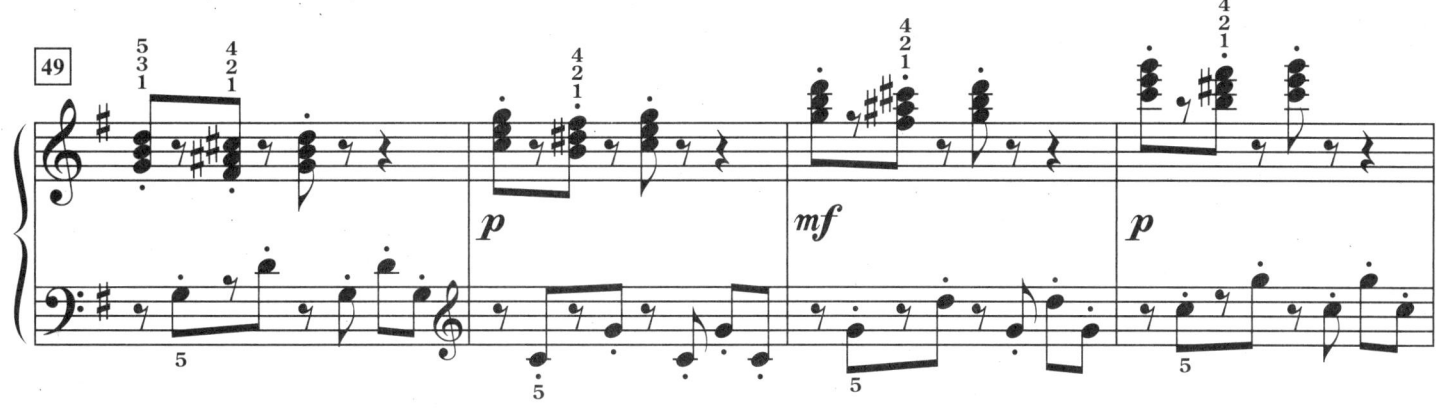

Toccata marcato*

Dennis Alexander

Vivace spirito (𝅗𝅥 = 104–112)

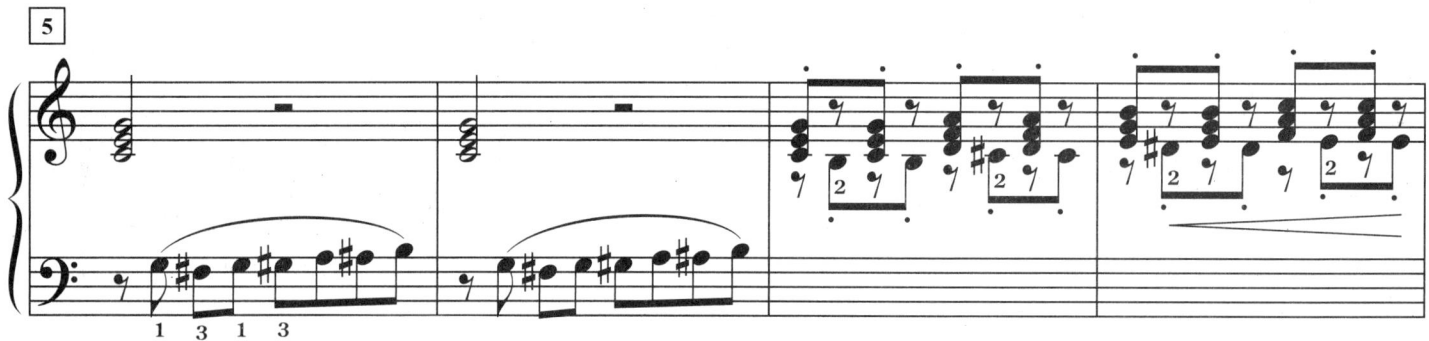

*Marcato = accented, stressed

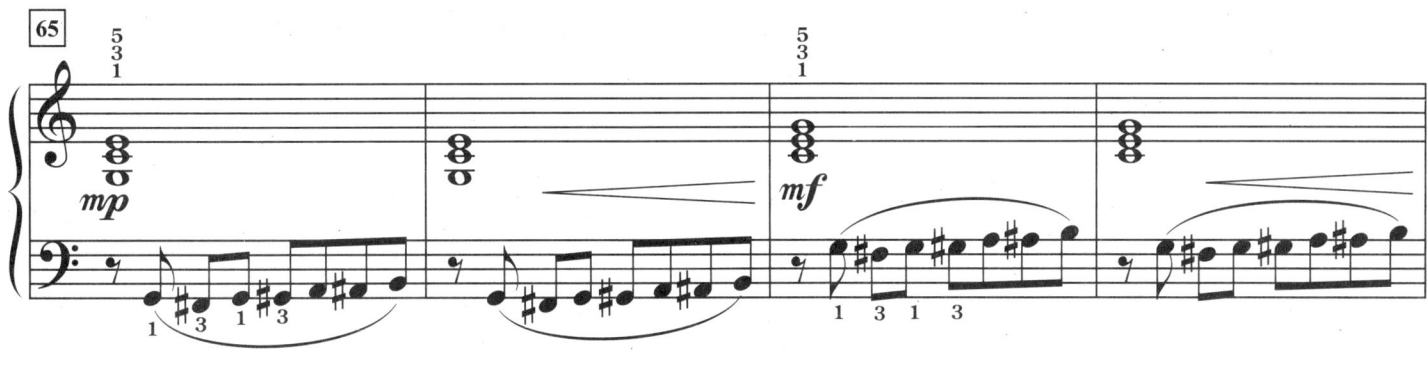

Toccata strepitoso*

Dennis Alexander

* Strepitoso = noisy, impetuous

Toccata alla breve*

Dennis Alexander

* Alla breve = cut time ($\mathbf{\complement} = \frac{2}{2}$)

Toccata fuoco*

Dennis Alexander

* Fuoco = fire

Toccata concitato*

Dennis Alexander

*Concitato = agitated

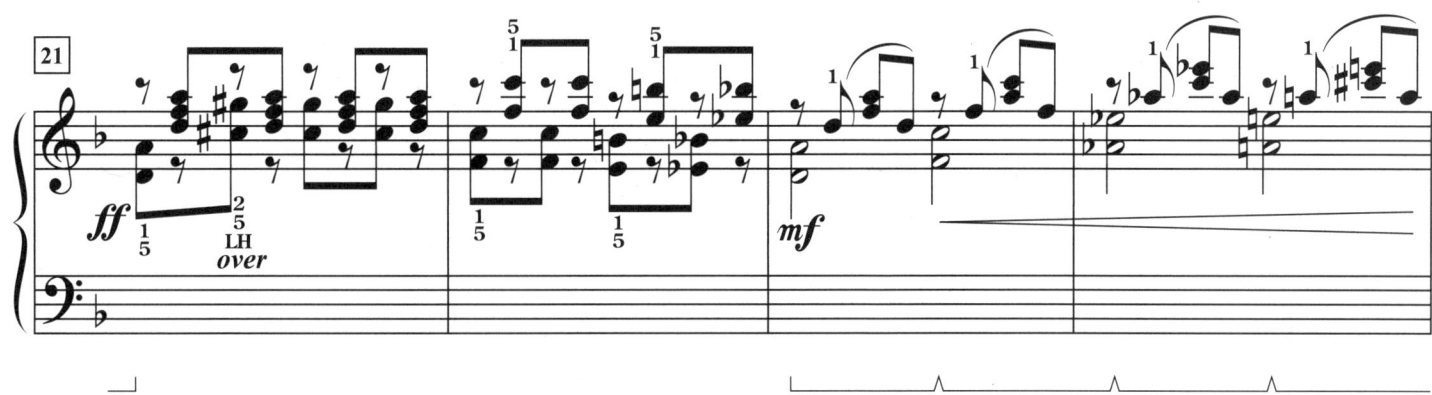
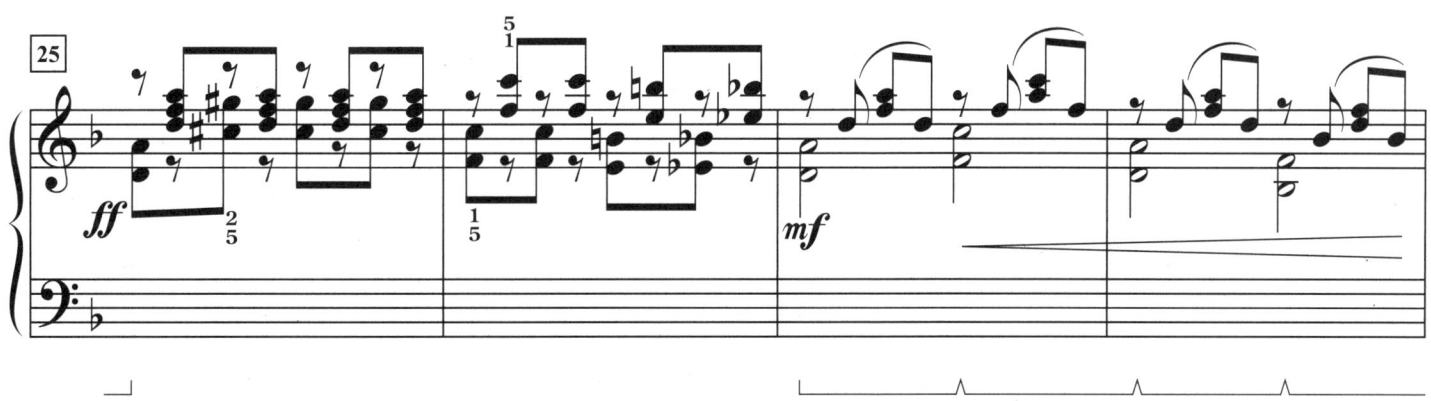
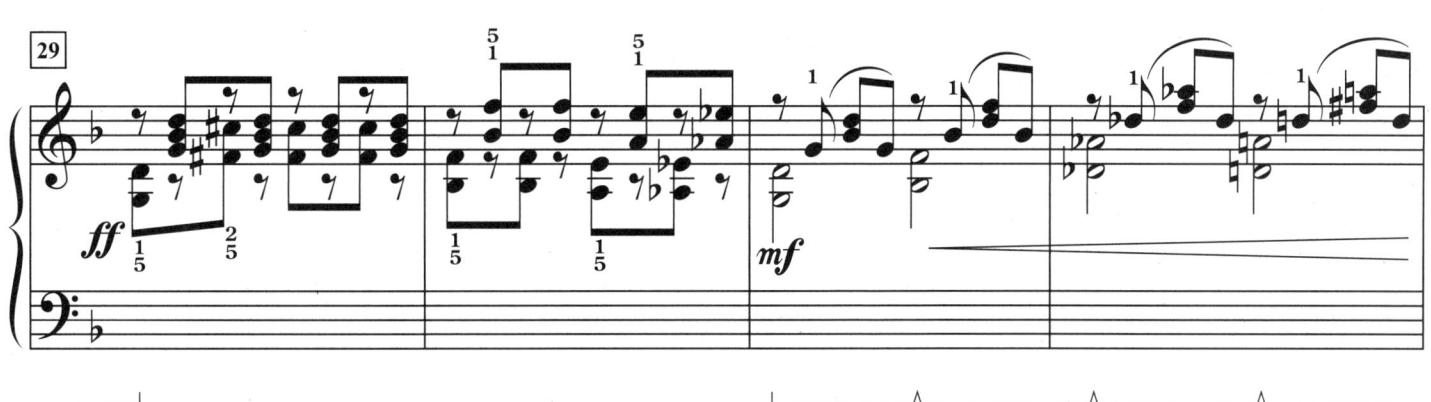

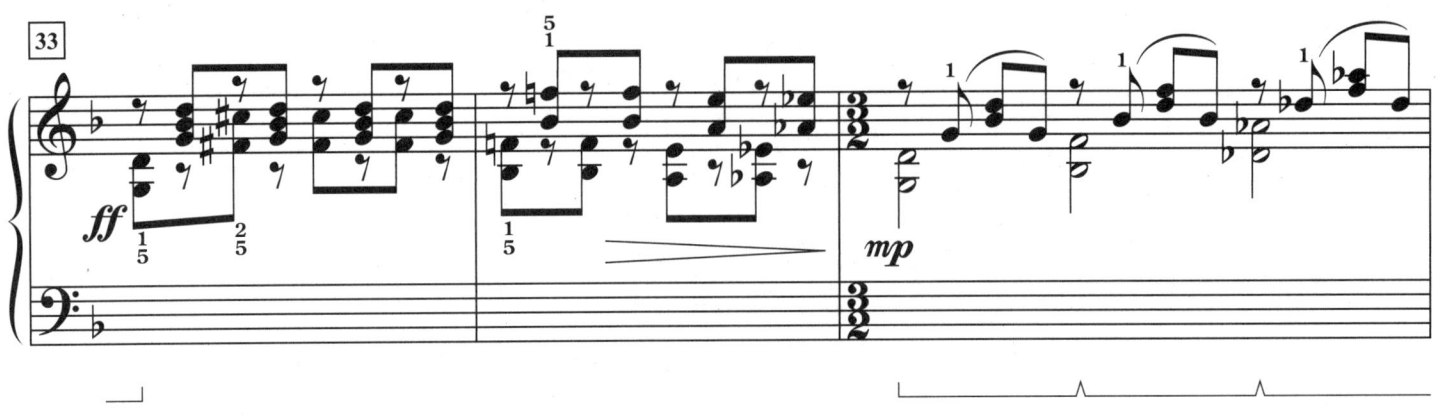

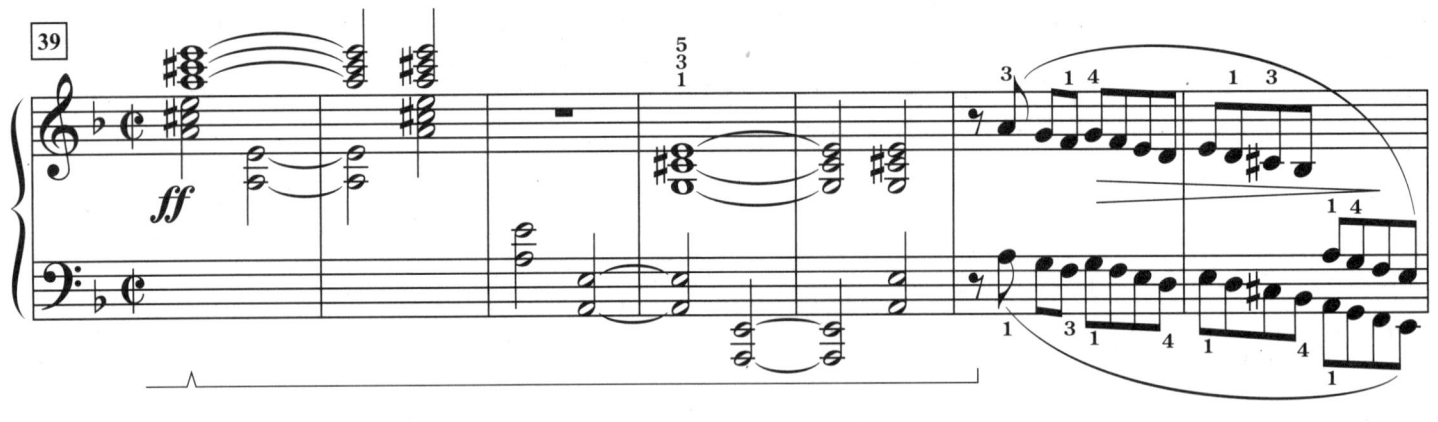
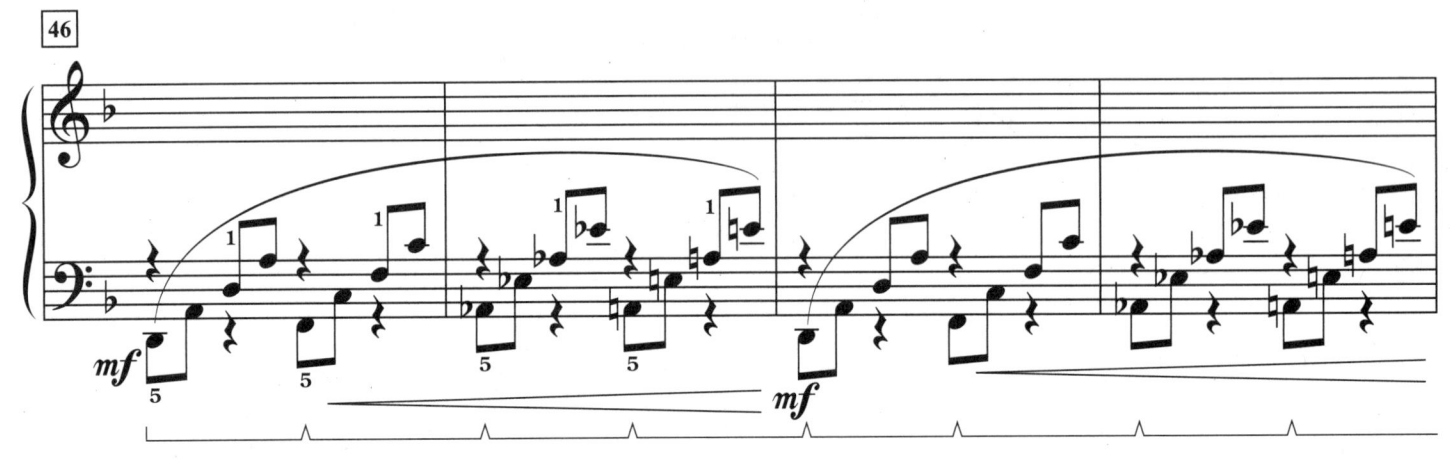

50
mp
f
54
mf
mf
58
f
LH
over
62
ff

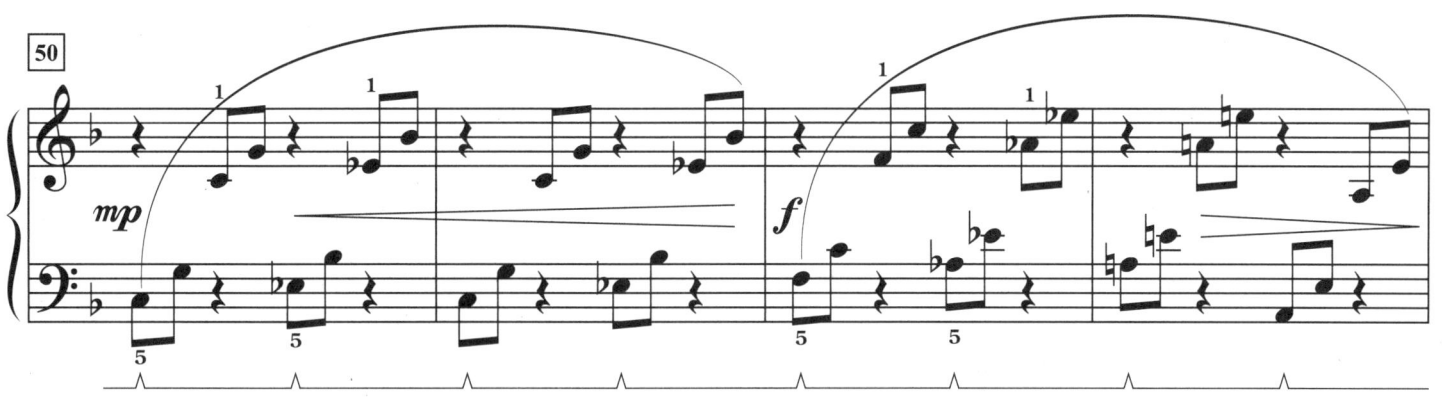

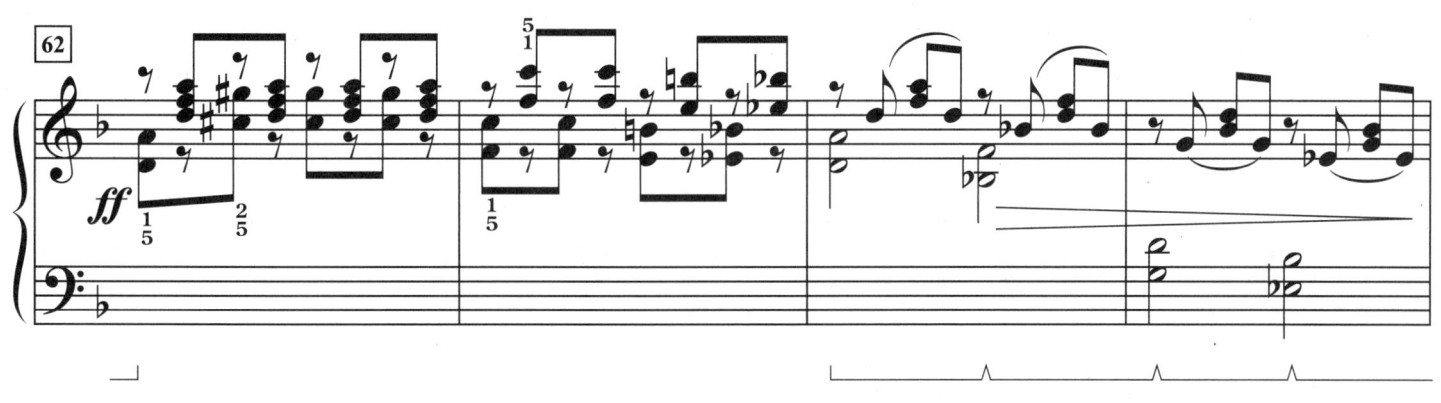

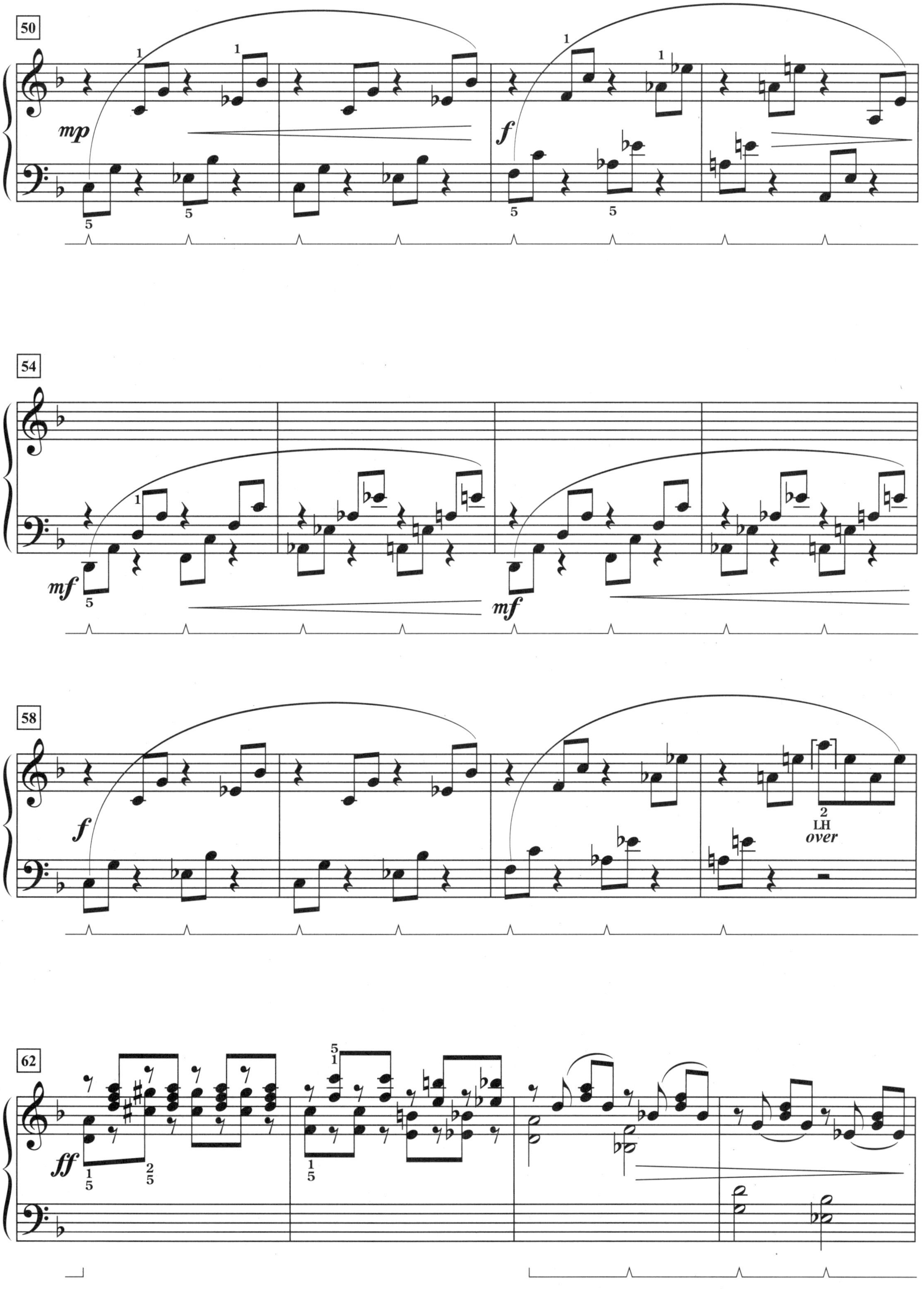

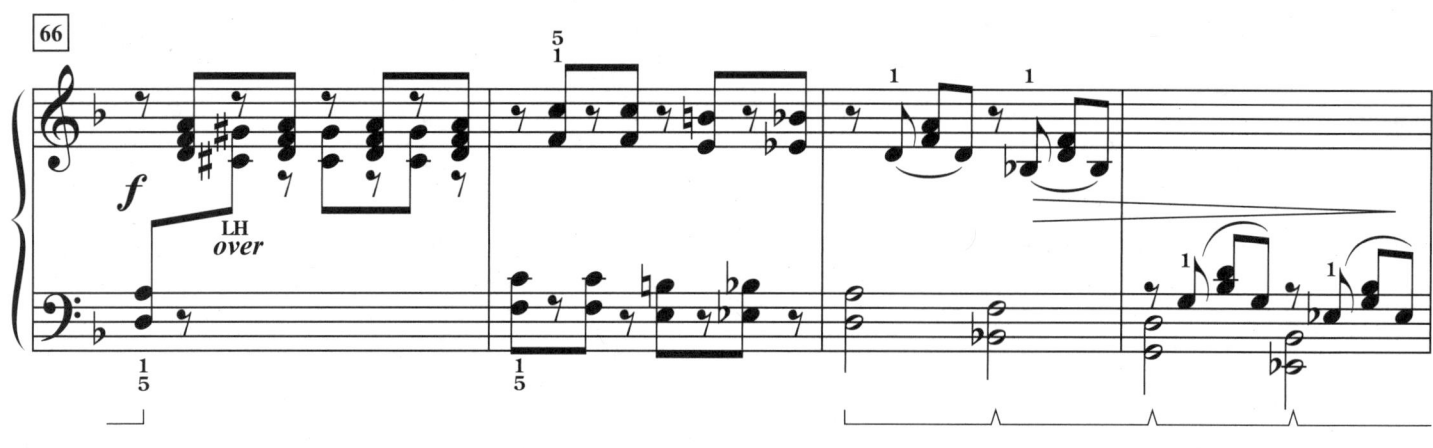

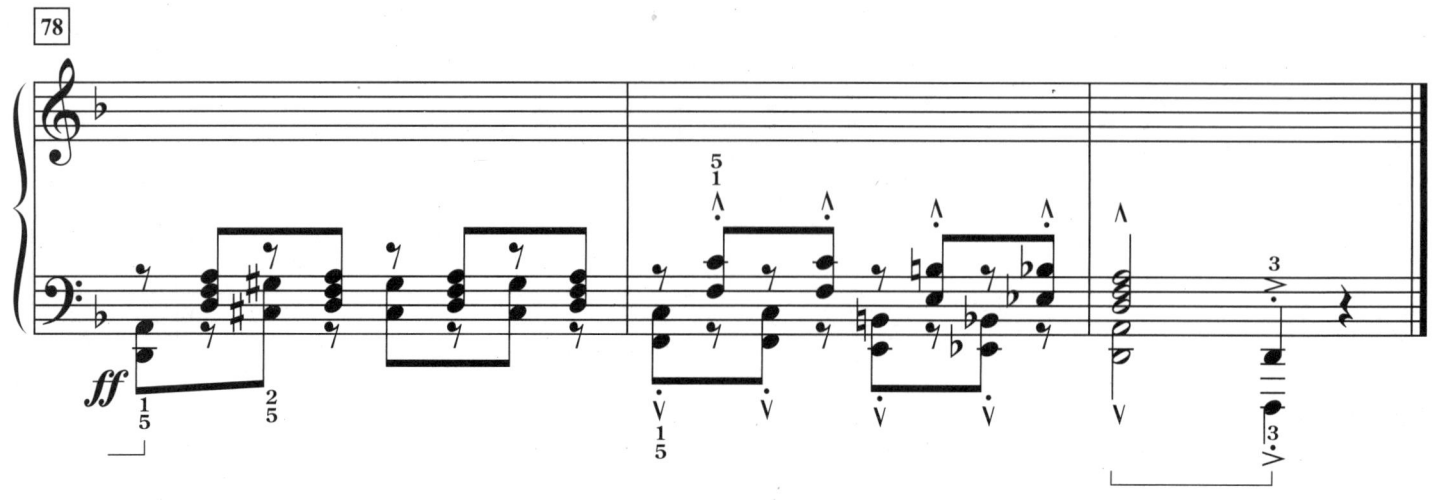